STUFF I CAN'T REMEMBER

BELONGS TO:

CYBER BOOKS INC

IF YOU LIKE THIS BOOK, PLEASE CONSIDER LEAVING A REVIEW ON AMAZON.
THANK YOU!

STUFF I CAN'T REMEMBER

Website	
Username	
Password	
Email	
Notes	

Website	
Username	
Password	
Email	
Notes	

Website	
Username	
Password	
Email	
Notes	

Website	
Username	
Password	
Email	
Notes	

Website	
Username	
Password	
Email	
Notes	

Website	
Username	
Password	
Email	
Notes	

Website	
Username	
Password	
Email	
Notes	

Website	
Username	
Password	
Email	
Notes	

STUFF I CAN'T REMEMBER

Website	
Username	
Password	
Email	
Notes	

Website	
Username	
Password	
Email	
Notes	

Website	
Username	
Password	
Email	
Notes	

Website	
Username	
Password	
Email	
Notes	

Website	
Username	
Password	
Email	
Notes	

Website	
Username	
Password	
Email	
Notes	

Website	
Username	
Password	
Email	
Notes	

Website	
Username	
Password	
Email	
Notes	

STUFF I CAN'T REMEMBER

Website	
Username	
Password	
Email	
Notes	

Website	
Username	
Password	
Email	
Notes	

Website	
Username	
Password	
Email	
Notes	

Website	
Username	
Password	
Email	
Notes	

Website	
Username	
Password	
Email	
Notes	

Website	
Username	
Password	
Email	
Notes	

Website	
Username	
Password	
Email	
Notes	

Website	
Username	
Password	
Email	
Notes	

STUFF I CAN'T REMEMBER

Website	
Username	
Password	
Email	
Notes	

Website	
Username	
Password	
Email	
Notes	

Website	
Username	
Password	
Email	
Notes	

Website	
Username	
Password	
Email	
Notes	

Website	
Username	
Password	
Email	
Notes	

Website	
Username	
Password	
Email	
Notes	

Website	
Username	
Password	
Email	
Notes	

Website	
Username	
Password	
Email	
Notes	

STUFF I CAN'T REMEMBER

A

Website	
Username	
Password	
Email	
Notes	

Website	
Username	
Password	
Email	
Notes	

Website	
Username	
Password	
Email	
Notes	

Website	
Username	
Password	
Email	
Notes	

Website	
Username	
Password	
Email	
Notes	

Website	
Username	
Password	
Email	
Notes	

Website	
Username	
Password	
Email	
Notes	

Website	
Username	
Password	
Email	
Notes	

STUFF I CAN'T REMEMBER

Website	
Username	
Password	
Email	
Notes	

Website	
Username	
Password	
Email	
Notes	

Website	
Username	
Password	
Email	
Notes	

Website	
Username	
Password	
Email	
Notes	

Website	
Username	
Password	
Email	
Notes	

Website	
Username	
Password	
Email	
Notes	

Website	
Username	
Password	
Email	
Notes	

Website	
Username	
Password	
Email	
Notes	

STUFF I CAN'T REMEMBER

B.

Website	
Username	
Password	
Email	
Notes	

Website	
Username	
Password	
Email	
Notes	

Website	
Username	
Password	
Email	
Notes	

Website	
Username	
Password	
Email	
Notes	

Website	
Username	
Password	
Email	
Notes	

Website	
Username	
Password	
Email	
Notes	

Website	
Username	
Password	
Email	
Notes	

Website	
Username	
Password	
Email	
Notes	

STUFF I CAN'T REMEMBER

Website	
Username	
Password	
Email	
Notes	

Website	
Username	
Password	
Email	
Notes	

Website	
Username	
Password	
Email	
Notes	

Website	
Username	
Password	
Email	
Notes	

Website	
Username	
Password	
Email	
Notes	

Website	
Username	
Password	
Email	
Notes	

Website	
Username	
Password	
Email	
Notes	

Website	
Username	
Password	
Email	
Notes	

STUFF I CAN'T REMEMBER

B

Website	
Username	
Password	
Email	
Notes	

Website	
Username	
Password	
Email	
Notes	

Website	
Username	
Password	
Email	
Notes	

Website	
Username	
Password	
Email	
Notes	

Website	
Username	
Password	
Email	
Notes	

Website	
Username	
Password	
Email	
Notes	

Website	
Username	
Password	
Email	
Notes	

Website	
Username	
Password	
Email	
Notes	

STUFF I CAN'T REMEMBER

Website	
Username	
Password	
Email	
Notes	

Website	
Username	
Password	
Email	
Notes	

Website	
Username	
Password	
Email	
Notes	

Website	
Username	
Password	
Email	
Notes	

Website	
Username	
Password	
Email	
Notes	

Website	
Username	
Password	
Email	
Notes	

Website	
Username	
Password	
Email	
Notes	

Website	
Username	
Password	
Email	
Notes	

STUFF I CAN'T REMEMBER

C

Website	
Username	5253 0200 0494 7918 / 983
Password	
Email	
Notes	12/22 - 02/27

Website	CREDIT CARD
Username	
Password	
Email	
Notes	

Website	
Username	Creative Homecare
Password	01324 827394
Email	
Notes	Support Staff : Jill & Roslyn

Website	
Username	
Password	c/ Jo Hall
Email	
Notes	

Website	
Username	
Password	
Email	
Notes	

Website	
Username	
Password	
Email	
Notes	

Website	
Username	
Password	
Email	
Notes	

Website	
Username	
Password	
Email	
Notes	

STUFF I CAN'T REMEMBER

Website	
Username	
Password	
Email	
Notes	

Website	
Username	
Password	
Email	
Notes	

Website	
Username	
Password	
Email	
Notes	

Website	
Username	
Password	
Email	
Notes	

Website	
Username	
Password	
Email	
Notes	

Website	
Username	
Password	
Email	
Notes	

Website	
Username	
Password	
Email	
Notes	

Website	
Username	
Password	
Email	
Notes	

C

STUFF I CAN'T REMEMBER

Website	
Username	
Password	
Email	
Notes	

Website	
Username	
Password	
Email	
Notes	

Website	
Username	
Password	
Email	
Notes	

Website	
Username	
Password	
Email	
Notes	

Website	
Username	
Password	
Email	
Notes	

Website	
Username	
Password	
Email	
Notes	

Website	
Username	
Password	
Email	
Notes	

Website	
Username	
Password	
Email	
Notes	

STUFF I CAN'T REMEMBER

Website	
Username	
Password	
Email	
Notes	

Website	
Username	
Password	
Email	
Notes	

Website	
Username	
Password	
Email	
Notes	

Website	
Username	
Password	
Email	
Notes	

Website	
Username	
Password	
Email	
Notes	

Website	
Username	
Password	
Email	
Notes	

Website	
Username	
Password	
Email	
Notes	

Website	
Username	
Password	
Email	
Notes	

STUFF I CAN'T REMEMBER

Website	
Username	
Password	
Email	
Notes	

Website	
Username	
Password	
Email	
Notes	

Website	
Username	
Password	
Email	
Notes	

Website	
Username	
Password	
Email	
Notes	

Website	
Username	
Password	
Email	
Notes	

Website	
Username	
Password	
Email	
Notes	

Website	
Username	
Password	
Email	
Notes	

Website	
Username	
Password	
Email	
Notes	

STUFF I CAN'T REMEMBER

Website	
Username	
Password	
Email	
Notes	

Website	
Username	
Password	
Email	
Notes	

Website	
Username	
Password	
Email	
Notes	

Website	
Username	
Password	
Email	
Notes	

Website	
Username	
Password	
Email	
Notes	

Website	
Username	
Password	
Email	
Notes	

Website	
Username	
Password	
Email	
Notes	

Website	
Username	
Password	
Email	
Notes	

STUFF I CAN'T REMEMBER

Website	
Username	
Password	
Email	
Notes	

Website	
Username	
Password	
Email	
Notes	

Website	
Username	
Password	
Email	
Notes	

Website	
Username	
Password	
Email	
Notes	

Website	
Username	
Password	
Email	
Notes	

Website	
Username	
Password	
Email	
Notes	

Website	
Username	
Password	
Email	
Notes	

Website	
Username	
Password	
Email	
Notes	

STUFF I CAN'T REMEMBER

Website	
Username	
Password	
Email	
Notes	

Website	
Username	
Password	
Email	
Notes	

Website	
Username	
Password	
Email	
Notes	

Website	
Username	
Password	
Email	
Notes	

Website	
Username	
Password	
Email	
Notes	

Website	
Username	
Password	
Email	
Notes	

Website	
Username	
Password	
Email	
Notes	

Website	
Username	
Password	
Email	
Notes	

STUFF I CAN'T REMEMBER

E

Website	
Username	
Password	
Email	
Notes	

Website	
Username	
Password	
Email	
Notes	

Website	
Username	
Password	
Email	
Notes	

Website	
Username	
Password	
Email	
Notes	

Website	
Username	
Password	
Email	
Notes	

Website	
Username	
Password	
Email	
Notes	

Website	
Username	
Password	
Email	
Notes	

Website	
Username	
Password	
Email	
Notes	

STUFF I CAN'T REMEMBER

Website	
Username	
Password	
Email	
Notes	

Website	
Username	
Password	
Email	
Notes	

Website	
Username	
Password	
Email	
Notes	

Website	
Username	
Password	
Email	
Notes	

Website	
Username	
Password	
Email	
Notes	

Website	
Username	
Password	
Email	
Notes	

Website	
Username	
Password	
Email	
Notes	

Website	
Username	
Password	
Email	
Notes	

STUFF I CAN'T REMEMBER

F

Website	
Username	
Password	
Email	
Notes	

Website	
Username	
Password	
Email	
Notes	

Website	
Username	
Password	
Email	
Notes	

Website	
Username	
Password	
Email	
Notes	

Website	
Username	
Password	
Email	
Notes	

Website	
Username	
Password	
Email	
Notes	

Website	
Username	
Password	
Email	
Notes	

Website	
Username	
Password	
Email	
Notes	

STUFF I CAN'T REMEMBER

Website	
Username	
Password	
Email	
Notes	

Website	
Username	
Password	
Email	
Notes	

Website	
Username	
Password	
Email	
Notes	

Website	
Username	
Password	
Email	
Notes	

Website	
Username	
Password	
Email	
Notes	

Website	
Username	
Password	
Email	
Notes	

Website	
Username	
Password	
Email	
Notes	

Website	
Username	
Password	
Email	
Notes	

STUFF I CAN'T REMEMBER

F

Website	
Username	
Password	
Email	
Notes	

Website	
Username	
Password	
Email	
Notes	

Website	
Username	
Password	
Email	
Notes	

Website	
Username	
Password	
Email	
Notes	

Website	
Username	
Password	
Email	
Notes	

Website	
Username	
Password	
Email	
Notes	

Website	
Username	
Password	
Email	
Notes	

Website	
Username	
Password	
Email	
Notes	

STUFF I CAN'T REMEMBER

Website	
Username	
Password	
Email	
Notes	

Website	
Username	
Password	
Email	
Notes	

Website	
Username	
Password	
Email	
Notes	

Website	
Username	
Password	
Email	
Notes	

Website	
Username	
Password	
Email	
Notes	

Website	
Username	
Password	
Email	
Notes	

Website	
Username	
Password	
Email	
Notes	

Website	
Username	
Password	
Email	
Notes	

STUFF I CAN'T REMEMBER

Website	
Username	
Password	
Email	
Notes	

Website	
Username	
Password	
Email	
Notes	

Website	
Username	
Password	
Email	
Notes	

Website	
Username	
Password	
Email	
Notes	

Website	
Username	
Password	
Email	
Notes	

Website	
Username	
Password	
Email	
Notes	

Website	
Username	
Password	
Email	
Notes	

Website	
Username	
Password	
Email	
Notes	

STUFF I CAN'T REMEMBER

Website	
Username	
Password	
Email	
Notes	

Website	
Username	
Password	
Email	
Notes	

Website	
Username	
Password	
Email	
Notes	

Website	
Username	
Password	
Email	
Notes	

Website	
Username	
Password	
Email	
Notes	

Website	
Username	
Password	
Email	
Notes	

Website	
Username	
Password	
Email	
Notes	

Website	
Username	
Password	
Email	
Notes	

STUFF I CAN'T REMEMBER

Website	
Username	
Password	
Email	
Notes	

Website	
Username	
Password	
Email	
Notes	

Website	
Username	
Password	
Email	
Notes	

Website	
Username	
Password	
Email	
Notes	

Website	
Username	
Password	
Email	
Notes	

Website	
Username	
Password	
Email	
Notes	

Website	
Username	
Password	
Email	
Notes	

Website	
Username	
Password	
Email	
Notes	

STUFF I CAN'T REMEMBER

Website	
Username	
Password	
Email	
Notes	

Website	
Username	
Password	
Email	
Notes	

Website	
Username	
Password	
Email	
Notes	

Website	
Username	
Password	
Email	
Notes	

Website	
Username	
Password	
Email	
Notes	

Website	
Username	
Password	
Email	
Notes	

Website	
Username	
Password	
Email	
Notes	

Website	
Username	
Password	
Email	
Notes	

STUFF I CAN'T REMEMBER

H

Website	
Username	JO HALL, Creative Homecare
Password	07917 703902
Email	
Notes	

Website	
Username	
Password	
Email	
Notes	

Website	
Username	
Password	
Email	
Notes	

Website	
Username	
Password	
Email	
Notes	

Website	
Username	
Password	
Email	
Notes	

Website	
Username	
Password	
Email	
Notes	

Website	
Username	
Password	
Email	
Notes	

Website	
Username	
Password	
Email	
Notes	

STUFF I CAN'T REMEMBER

Website	
Username	
Password	
Email	
Notes	

Website	
Username	
Password	
Email	
Notes	

Website	
Username	
Password	
Email	
Notes	

Website	
Username	
Password	
Email	
Notes	

Website	
Username	
Password	
Email	
Notes	

Website	
Username	
Password	
Email	
Notes	

Website	
Username	
Password	
Email	
Notes	

Website	
Username	
Password	
Email	
Notes	

STUFF I CAN'T REMEMBER

H

Website	
Username	
Password	
Email	
Notes	

Website	
Username	
Password	
Email	
Notes	

Website	
Username	
Password	
Email	
Notes	

Website	
Username	
Password	
Email	
Notes	

Website	
Username	
Password	
Email	
Notes	

Website	
Username	
Password	
Email	
Notes	

Website	
Username	
Password	
Email	
Notes	

Website	
Username	
Password	
Email	
Notes	

STUFF I CAN'T REMEMBER

Website	
Username	
Password	
Email	
Notes	

Website	
Username	
Password	
Email	
Notes	

Website	
Username	
Password	
Email	
Notes	

Website	
Username	
Password	
Email	
Notes	

Website	
Username	
Password	
Email	
Notes	

Website	
Username	
Password	
Email	
Notes	

Website	
Username	
Password	
Email	
Notes	

Website	
Username	
Password	
Email	
Notes	

STUFF I CAN'T REMEMBER

Website	
Username	
Password	
Email	
Notes	

Website	
Username	
Password	
Email	
Notes	

Website	
Username	
Password	
Email	
Notes	

Website	
Username	
Password	
Email	
Notes	

Website	
Username	
Password	
Email	
Notes	

Website	
Username	
Password	
Email	
Notes	

Website	
Username	
Password	
Email	
Notes	

Website	
Username	
Password	
Email	
Notes	

STUFF I CAN'T REMEMBER

Website	
Username	
Password	
Email	
Notes	

Website	
Username	
Password	
Email	
Notes	

Website	
Username	
Password	
Email	
Notes	

Website	
Username	
Password	
Email	
Notes	

Website	
Username	
Password	
Email	
Notes	

Website	
Username	
Password	
Email	
Notes	

Website	
Username	
Password	
Email	
Notes	

Website	
Username	
Password	
Email	
Notes	

STUFF I CAN'T REMEMBER

Website	
Username	
Password	
Email	
Notes	

Website	
Username	
Password	
Email	
Notes	

Website	
Username	
Password	
Email	
Notes	

Website	
Username	
Password	
Email	
Notes	

Website	
Username	
Password	
Email	
Notes	

Website	
Username	
Password	
Email	
Notes	

Website	
Username	
Password	
Email	
Notes	

Website	
Username	
Password	
Email	
Notes	

STUFF I CAN'T REMEMBER

Website	
Username	
Password	
Email	
Notes	

Website	
Username	
Password	
Email	
Notes	

Website	
Username	
Password	
Email	
Notes	

Website	
Username	
Password	
Email	
Notes	

Website	
Username	
Password	
Email	
Notes	

Website	
Username	
Password	
Email	
Notes	

Website	
Username	
Password	
Email	
Notes	

Website	
Username	
Password	
Email	
Notes	

STUFF I CAN'T REMEMBER

J

Website	
Username	
Password	
Email	
Notes	

Website	
Username	
Password	
Email	
Notes	

Website	
Username	
Password	
Email	
Notes	

Website	
Username	
Password	
Email	
Notes	

Website	
Username	
Password	
Email	
Notes	

Website	
Username	
Password	
Email	
Notes	

Website	
Username	
Password	
Email	
Notes	

Website	
Username	
Password	
Email	
Notes	

STUFF I CAN'T REMEMBER

Website	
Username	
Password	
Email	
Notes	

Website	
Username	
Password	
Email	
Notes	

Website	
Username	
Password	
Email	
Notes	

Website	
Username	
Password	
Email	
Notes	

Website	
Username	
Password	
Email	
Notes	

Website	
Username	
Password	
Email	
Notes	

Website	
Username	
Password	
Email	
Notes	

Website	
Username	
Password	
Email	
Notes	

STUFF I CAN'T REMEMBER

J

Website	
Username	
Password	
Email	
Notes	

Website	
Username	
Password	
Email	
Notes	

Website	
Username	
Password	
Email	
Notes	

Website	
Username	
Password	
Email	
Notes	

Website	
Username	
Password	
Email	
Notes	

Website	
Username	
Password	
Email	
Notes	

Website	
Username	
Password	
Email	
Notes	

Website	
Username	
Password	
Email	
Notes	

STUFF I CAN'T REMEMBER

Website	
Username	
Password	
Email	
Notes	

Website	
Username	
Password	
Email	
Notes	

Website	
Username	
Password	
Email	
Notes	

Website	
Username	
Password	
Email	
Notes	

Website	
Username	
Password	
Email	
Notes	

Website	
Username	
Password	
Email	
Notes	

Website	
Username	
Password	
Email	
Notes	

Website	
Username	
Password	
Email	
Notes	

STUFF I CAN'T REMEMBER

K

Website	
Username	
Password	
Email	
Notes	

Website	
Username	
Password	
Email	
Notes	

Website	
Username	
Password	
Email	
Notes	

Website	
Username	
Password	
Email	
Notes	

Website	
Username	
Password	
Email	
Notes	

Website	
Username	
Password	
Email	
Notes	

Website	
Username	
Password	
Email	
Notes	

Website	
Username	
Password	
Email	
Notes	

STUFF I CAN'T REMEMBER

Website	
Username	
Password	
Email	
Notes	

Website	
Username	
Password	
Email	
Notes	

Website	
Username	
Password	
Email	
Notes	

Website	
Username	
Password	
Email	
Notes	

Website	
Username	
Password	
Email	
Notes	

Website	
Username	
Password	
Email	
Notes	

Website	
Username	
Password	
Email	
Notes	

Website	
Username	
Password	
Email	
Notes	

STUFF I CAN'T REMEMBER

K

Website	
Username	
Password	
Email	
Notes	

Website	
Username	
Password	
Email	
Notes	

Website	
Username	
Password	
Email	
Notes	

Website	
Username	
Password	
Email	
Notes	

Website	
Username	
Password	
Email	
Notes	

Website	
Username	
Password	
Email	
Notes	

Website	
Username	
Password	
Email	
Notes	

Website	
Username	
Password	
Email	
Notes	

STUFF I CAN'T REMEMBER

Website	
Username	
Password	
Email	
Notes	

Website	
Username	
Password	
Email	
Notes	

Website	
Username	
Password	
Email	
Notes	

Website	
Username	
Password	
Email	
Notes	

Website	
Username	
Password	
Email	
Notes	

Website	
Username	
Password	
Email	
Notes	

Website	
Username	
Password	
Email	
Notes	

Website	
Username	
Password	
Email	
Notes	

STUFF I CAN'T REMEMBER

L

Website	
Username	
Password	
Email	
Notes	

Website	
Username	
Password	
Email	
Notes	

Website	
Username	
Password	
Email	
Notes	

Website	
Username	
Password	
Email	
Notes	

Website	
Username	
Password	
Email	
Notes	

Website	
Username	
Password	
Email	
Notes	

Website	
Username	
Password	
Email	
Notes	

Website	
Username	
Password	
Email	
Notes	

STUFF I CAN'T REMEMBER

Website	
Username	
Password	
Email	
Notes	

Website	
Username	
Password	
Email	
Notes	

Website	
Username	
Password	
Email	
Notes	

Website	
Username	
Password	
Email	
Notes	

Website	
Username	
Password	
Email	
Notes	

Website	
Username	
Password	
Email	
Notes	

Website	
Username	
Password	
Email	
Notes	

Website	
Username	
Password	
Email	
Notes	

STUFF I CAN'T REMEMBER

L

Website	
Username	
Password	
Email	
Notes	

Website	
Username	
Password	
Email	
Notes	

Website	
Username	
Password	
Email	
Notes	

Website	
Username	
Password	
Email	
Notes	

Website	
Username	
Password	
Email	
Notes	

Website	
Username	
Password	
Email	
Notes	

Website	
Username	
Password	
Email	
Notes	

Website	
Username	
Password	
Email	
Notes	

STUFF I CAN'T REMEMBER

Website	
Username	
Password	
Email	
Notes	

Website	
Username	
Password	
Email	
Notes	

Website	
Username	
Password	
Email	
Notes	

Website	
Username	
Password	
Email	
Notes	

Website	
Username	
Password	
Email	
Notes	

Website	
Username	
Password	
Email	
Notes	

Website	
Username	
Password	
Email	
Notes	

Website	
Username	
Password	
Email	
Notes	

STUFF I CAN'T REMEMBER

M

Website	
Username	
Password	
Email	
Notes	

Website	
Username	
Password	
Email	
Notes	

Website	
Username	
Password	
Email	
Notes	

Website	
Username	
Password	
Email	
Notes	

Website	
Username	
Password	
Email	
Notes	

Website	
Username	
Password	
Email	
Notes	

Website	
Username	
Password	
Email	
Notes	

Website	
Username	
Password	
Email	
Notes	

STUFF I CAN'T REMEMBER

Website	
Username	
Password	
Email	
Notes	

Website	
Username	
Password	
Email	
Notes	

Website	
Username	
Password	
Email	
Notes	

Website	
Username	
Password	
Email	
Notes	

Website	
Username	
Password	
Email	
Notes	

Website	
Username	
Password	
Email	
Notes	

Website	
Username	
Password	
Email	
Notes	

Website	
Username	
Password	
Email	
Notes	

STUFF I CAN'T REMEMBER

M

Website	
Username	
Password	
Email	
Notes	

Website	
Username	
Password	
Email	
Notes	

Website	
Username	
Password	
Email	
Notes	

Website	
Username	
Password	
Email	
Notes	

Website	
Username	
Password	
Email	
Notes	

Website	
Username	
Password	
Email	
Notes	

Website	
Username	
Password	
Email	
Notes	

Website	
Username	
Password	
Email	
Notes	

STUFF I CAN'T REMEMBER

Website	
Username	
Password	
Email	
Notes	

Website	
Username	
Password	
Email	
Notes	

Website	
Username	
Password	
Email	
Notes	

Website	
Username	
Password	
Email	
Notes	

Website	
Username	
Password	
Email	
Notes	

Website	
Username	
Password	
Email	
Notes	

Website	
Username	
Password	
Email	
Notes	

Website	
Username	
Password	
Email	
Notes	

STUFF I CAN'T REMEMBER

N

Website	
Username	
Password	
Email	
Notes	

Website	
Username	
Password	
Email	
Notes	

Website	
Username	
Password	
Email	
Notes	

Website	
Username	
Password	
Email	
Notes	

Website	
Username	
Password	
Email	
Notes	

Website	
Username	
Password	
Email	
Notes	

Website	
Username	
Password	
Email	
Notes	

Website	
Username	
Password	
Email	
Notes	

STUFF I CAN'T REMEMBER

Website	
Username	
Password	
Email	
Notes	

Website	
Username	
Password	
Email	
Notes	

Website	
Username	
Password	
Email	
Notes	

Website	
Username	
Password	
Email	
Notes	

Website	
Username	
Password	
Email	
Notes	

Website	
Username	
Password	
Email	
Notes	

Website	
Username	
Password	
Email	
Notes	

Website	
Username	
Password	
Email	
Notes	

STUFF I CAN'T REMEMBER

N

Website	
Username	
Password	
Email	
Notes	

Website	
Username	
Password	
Email	
Notes	

Website	
Username	
Password	
Email	
Notes	

Website	
Username	
Password	
Email	
Notes	

Website	
Username	
Password	
Email	
Notes	

Website	
Username	
Password	
Email	
Notes	

Website	
Username	
Password	
Email	
Notes	

Website	
Username	
Password	
Email	
Notes	

STUFF I CAN'T REMEMBER

Website	
Username	
Password	
Email	
Notes	

Website	
Username	
Password	
Email	
Notes	

Website	
Username	
Password	
Email	
Notes	

Website	
Username	
Password	
Email	
Notes	

Website	
Username	
Password	
Email	
Notes	

Website	
Username	
Password	
Email	
Notes	

Website	
Username	
Password	
Email	
Notes	

Website	
Username	
Password	
Email	
Notes	

STUFF I CAN'T REMEMBER

O

Website	
Username	Oats-So-Simple Mix + 51ml water
Password	
Email	
Notes	

Website	
Username	
Password	
Email	
Notes	

Website	
Username	
Password	
Email	
Notes	

Website	
Username	
Password	
Email	
Notes	

Website	
Username	
Password	
Email	
Notes	

Website	
Username	
Password	
Email	
Notes	

Website	
Username	
Password	
Email	
Notes	

Website	
Username	
Password	
Email	
Notes	

STUFF I CAN'T REMEMBER

Website	
Username	
Password	
Email	
Notes	

Website	
Username	
Password	
Email	
Notes	

Website	
Username	
Password	
Email	
Notes	

Website	
Username	
Password	
Email	
Notes	

Website	
Username	
Password	
Email	
Notes	

Website	
Username	
Password	
Email	
Notes	

Website	
Username	
Password	
Email	
Notes	

Website	
Username	
Password	
Email	
Notes	

STUFF I CAN'T REMEMBER

Website	
Username	
Password	
Email	
Notes	

Website	
Username	
Password	
Email	
Notes	

Website	
Username	
Password	
Email	
Notes	

Website	
Username	
Password	
Email	
Notes	

Website	
Username	
Password	
Email	
Notes	

Website	
Username	
Password	
Email	
Notes	

Website	
Username	
Password	
Email	
Notes	

Website	
Username	
Password	
Email	
Notes	

STUFF I CAN'T REMEMBER

Website	
Username	
Password	
Email	
Notes	

Website	
Username	
Password	
Email	
Notes	

Website	
Username	
Password	
Email	
Notes	

Website	
Username	
Password	
Email	
Notes	

Website	
Username	
Password	
Email	
Notes	

Website	
Username	
Password	
Email	
Notes	

Website	
Username	
Password	
Email	
Notes	

Website	
Username	
Password	
Email	
Notes	

STUFF I CAN'T REMEMBER

P

Pension wef 1 April 2023:
£30499.96, i.e £2541.63 per month

Website	
Username	
Password	
Email	
Notes	

Website	
Username	
Password	
Email	
Notes	

Website	
Username	
Password	
Email	
Notes	

Website	
Username	
Password	
Email	
Notes	

Website	
Username	
Password	
Email	
Notes	

Website	
Username	
Password	
Email	
Notes	

Website	
Username	
Password	
Email	
Notes	

Website	
Username	
Password	
Email	
Notes	

STUFF I CAN'T REMEMBER

Website	
Username	
Password	
Email	
Notes	

Website	
Username	
Password	
Email	
Notes	

Website	
Username	
Password	
Email	
Notes	

Website	
Username	
Password	
Email	
Notes	

Website	
Username	
Password	
Email	
Notes	

Website	
Username	
Password	
Email	
Notes	

Website	
Username	
Password	
Email	
Notes	

Website	
Username	
Password	
Email	
Notes	

STUFF I CAN'T REMEMBER

P

Website	
Username	
Password	
Email	
Notes	

Website	
Username	
Password	
Email	
Notes	

Website	
Username	
Password	
Email	
Notes	

Website	
Username	
Password	
Email	
Notes	

Website	
Username	
Password	
Email	
Notes	

Website	
Username	
Password	
Email	
Notes	

Website	
Username	
Password	
Email	
Notes	

Website	
Username	
Password	
Email	
Notes	

STUFF I CAN'T REMEMBER

Website	
Username	
Password	
Email	
Notes	

Website	
Username	
Password	
Email	
Notes	

Website	
Username	
Password	
Email	
Notes	

Website	
Username	
Password	
Email	
Notes	

Website	
Username	
Password	
Email	
Notes	

Website	
Username	
Password	
Email	
Notes	

Website	
Username	
Password	
Email	
Notes	

Website	
Username	
Password	
Email	
Notes	

STUFF I CAN'T REMEMBER

Website	
Username	
Password	
Email	
Notes	

Website	
Username	
Password	
Email	
Notes	

Website	
Username	
Password	
Email	
Notes	

Website	
Username	
Password	
Email	
Notes	

Website	
Username	
Password	
Email	
Notes	

Website	
Username	
Password	
Email	
Notes	

Website	
Username	
Password	
Email	
Notes	

Website	
Username	
Password	
Email	
Notes	

STUFF I CAN'T REMEMBER

Website	
Username	
Password	
Email	
Notes	

Website	
Username	
Password	
Email	
Notes	

Website	
Username	
Password	
Email	
Notes	

Website	
Username	
Password	
Email	
Notes	

Website	
Username	
Password	
Email	
Notes	

Website	
Username	
Password	
Email	
Notes	

Website	
Username	
Password	
Email	
Notes	

Website	
Username	
Password	
Email	
Notes	

STUFF I CAN'T REMEMBER

Website	
Username	
Password	
Email	
Notes	

Website	
Username	
Password	
Email	
Notes	

Website	
Username	
Password	
Email	
Notes	

Website	
Username	
Password	
Email	
Notes	

Website	
Username	
Password	
Email	
Notes	

Website	
Username	
Password	
Email	
Notes	

Website	
Username	
Password	
Email	
Notes	

Website	
Username	
Password	
Email	
Notes	

STUFF I CAN'T REMEMBER

Website	
Username	
Password	
Email	
Notes	

Website	
Username	
Password	
Email	
Notes	

Website	
Username	
Password	
Email	
Notes	

Website	
Username	
Password	
Email	
Notes	

Website	
Username	
Password	
Email	
Notes	

Website	
Username	
Password	
Email	
Notes	

Website	
Username	
Password	
Email	
Notes	

Website	
Username	
Password	
Email	
Notes	

STUFF I CAN'T REMEMBER

R

Website	
Username	
Password	
Email	
Notes	

Website	
Username	
Password	
Email	
Notes	

Website	
Username	
Password	
Email	
Notes	

Website	
Username	
Password	
Email	
Notes	

Website	
Username	
Password	
Email	
Notes	

Website	
Username	
Password	
Email	
Notes	

Website	
Username	
Password	
Email	
Notes	

Website	
Username	
Password	
Email	
Notes	

STUFF I CAN'T REMEMBER

Website	
Username	
Password	
Email	
Notes	

Website	
Username	
Password	
Email	
Notes	

Website	
Username	
Password	
Email	
Notes	

Website	
Username	
Password	
Email	
Notes	

Website	
Username	
Password	
Email	
Notes	

Website	
Username	
Password	
Email	
Notes	

Website	
Username	
Password	
Email	
Notes	

Website	
Username	
Password	
Email	
Notes	

STUFF I CAN'T REMEMBER

7

Website	
Username	
Password	
Email	
Notes	

Website	
Username	
Password	
Email	
Notes	

Website	
Username	
Password	
Email	
Notes	

Website	
Username	
Password	
Email	
Notes	

Website	
Username	
Password	
Email	
Notes	

Website	
Username	
Password	
Email	
Notes	

Website	
Username	
Password	
Email	
Notes	

Website	
Username	
Password	
Email	
Notes	

STUFF I CAN'T REMEMBER

Website	
Username	
Password	
Email	
Notes	

Website	
Username	
Password	
Email	
Notes	

Website	
Username	
Password	
Email	
Notes	

Website	
Username	
Password	
Email	
Notes	

Website	
Username	
Password	
Email	
Notes	

Website	
Username	
Password	
Email	
Notes	

Website	
Username	
Password	
Email	
Notes	

Website	
Username	
Password	
Email	
Notes	

STUFF I CAN'T REMEMBER

Website	SOCPF
Username	Shell Overseas Contributory Pension Fund
Password	SOCPF 2121459
Email	
Notes	

Website	
Username	
Password	
Email	
Notes	

Website	
Username	
Password	
Email	
Notes	

Website	
Username	
Password	
Email	
Notes	

Website	
Username	
Password	
Email	
Notes	

Website	
Username	
Password	
Email	
Notes	

Website	
Username	
Password	
Email	
Notes	

Website	
Username	
Password	
Email	
Notes	

STUFF I CAN'T REMEMBER

Website	
Username	
Password	
Email	
Notes	

Website	
Username	
Password	
Email	
Notes	

Website	
Username	
Password	
Email	
Notes	

Website	
Username	
Password	
Email	
Notes	

Website	
Username	
Password	
Email	
Notes	

Website	
Username	
Password	
Email	
Notes	

Website	
Username	
Password	
Email	
Notes	

Website	
Username	
Password	
Email	
Notes	

STUFF I CAN'T REMEMBER

Website	
Username	
Password	
Email	
Notes	

Website	
Username	
Password	
Email	
Notes	

Website	
Username	
Password	
Email	
Notes	

Website	
Username	
Password	
Email	
Notes	

Website	
Username	
Password	
Email	
Notes	

Website	
Username	
Password	
Email	
Notes	

Website	
Username	
Password	
Email	
Notes	

Website	
Username	
Password	
Email	
Notes	

STUFF I CAN'T REMEMBER

Website	
Username	
Password	
Email	
Notes	

Website	
Username	
Password	
Email	
Notes	

Website	
Username	
Password	
Email	
Notes	

Website	
Username	
Password	
Email	
Notes	

Website	
Username	
Password	
Email	
Notes	

Website	
Username	
Password	
Email	
Notes	

Website	
Username	
Password	
Email	
Notes	

Website	
Username	
Password	
Email	
Notes	

STUFF I CAN'T REMEMBER

T

Website	
Username	
Password	
Email	
Notes	

Website	
Username	
Password	
Email	
Notes	

Website	
Username	
Password	
Email	
Notes	

Website	
Username	
Password	
Email	
Notes	

Website	
Username	
Password	
Email	
Notes	

Website	
Username	
Password	
Email	
Notes	

Website	
Username	
Password	
Email	
Notes	

Website	
Username	
Password	
Email	
Notes	

STUFF I CAN'T REMEMBER

Website	
Username	
Password	
Email	
Notes	

Website	
Username	
Password	
Email	
Notes	

Website	
Username	
Password	
Email	
Notes	

Website	
Username	
Password	
Email	
Notes	

Website	
Username	
Password	
Email	
Notes	

Website	
Username	
Password	
Email	
Notes	

Website	
Username	
Password	
Email	
Notes	

Website	
Username	
Password	
Email	
Notes	

STUFF I CAN'T REMEMBER

T

Website	
Username	
Password	
Email	
Notes	

Website	
Username	
Password	
Email	
Notes	

Website	
Username	
Password	
Email	
Notes	

Website	
Username	
Password	
Email	
Notes	

Website	
Username	
Password	
Email	
Notes	

Website	
Username	
Password	
Email	
Notes	

Website	
Username	
Password	
Email	
Notes	

Website	
Username	
Password	
Email	
Notes	

STUFF I CAN'T REMEMBER

Website	
Username	
Password	
Email	
Notes	

Website	
Username	
Password	
Email	
Notes	

Website	
Username	
Password	
Email	
Notes	

Website	
Username	
Password	
Email	
Notes	

Website	
Username	
Password	
Email	
Notes	

Website	
Username	
Password	
Email	
Notes	

Website	
Username	
Password	
Email	
Notes	

Website	
Username	
Password	
Email	
Notes	

U

STUFF I CAN'T REMEMBER

Website	
Username	
Password	
Email	
Notes	

Website	
Username	
Password	
Email	
Notes	

Website	
Username	
Password	
Email	
Notes	

Website	
Username	
Password	
Email	
Notes	

Website	
Username	
Password	
Email	
Notes	

Website	
Username	
Password	
Email	
Notes	

Website	
Username	
Password	
Email	
Notes	

Website	
Username	
Password	
Email	
Notes	

STUFF I CAN'T REMEMBER

Website	
Username	
Password	
Email	
Notes	

Website	
Username	
Password	
Email	
Notes	

Website	
Username	
Password	
Email	
Notes	

Website	
Username	
Password	
Email	
Notes	

Website	
Username	
Password	
Email	
Notes	

Website	
Username	
Password	
Email	
Notes	

Website	
Username	
Password	
Email	
Notes	

Website	
Username	
Password	
Email	
Notes	

STUFF I CAN'T REMEMBER

Website	
Username	
Password	
Email	
Notes	

Website	
Username	
Password	
Email	
Notes	

Website	
Username	
Password	
Email	
Notes	

Website	
Username	
Password	
Email	
Notes	

Website	
Username	
Password	
Email	
Notes	

Website	
Username	
Password	
Email	
Notes	

Website	
Username	
Password	
Email	
Notes	

Website	
Username	
Password	
Email	
Notes	

STUFF I CAN'T REMEMBER

Website	
Username	
Password	
Email	
Notes	

Website	
Username	
Password	
Email	
Notes	

Website	
Username	
Password	
Email	
Notes	

Website	
Username	
Password	
Email	
Notes	

Website	
Username	
Password	
Email	
Notes	

Website	
Username	
Password	
Email	
Notes	

Website	
Username	
Password	
Email	
Notes	

Website	
Username	
Password	
Email	
Notes	

STUFF I CAN'T REMEMBER

V

Website	
Username	
Password	
Email	
Notes	

Website	
Username	
Password	
Email	
Notes	

Website	
Username	
Password	
Email	
Notes	

Website	
Username	
Password	
Email	
Notes	

Website	
Username	
Password	
Email	
Notes	

Website	
Username	
Password	
Email	
Notes	

Website	
Username	
Password	
Email	
Notes	

Website	
Username	
Password	
Email	
Notes	

STUFF I CAN'T REMEMBER

Website	
Username	
Password	
Email	
Notes	

Website	
Username	
Password	
Email	
Notes	

Website	
Username	
Password	
Email	
Notes	

Website	
Username	
Password	
Email	
Notes	

Website	
Username	
Password	
Email	
Notes	

Website	
Username	
Password	
Email	
Notes	

Website	
Username	
Password	
Email	
Notes	

Website	
Username	
Password	
Email	
Notes	

STUFF I CAN'T REMEMBER

y

Website	
Username	
Password	
Email	
Notes	

Website	
Username	
Password	
Email	
Notes	

Website	
Username	
Password	
Email	
Notes	

Website	
Username	
Password	
Email	
Notes	

Website	
Username	
Password	
Email	
Notes	

Website	
Username	
Password	
Email	
Notes	

Website	
Username	
Password	
Email	
Notes	

Website	
Username	
Password	
Email	
Notes	

STUFF I CAN'T REMEMBER

Website	
Username	
Password	
Email	
Notes	

Website	
Username	
Password	
Email	
Notes	

Website	
Username	
Password	
Email	
Notes	

Website	
Username	
Password	
Email	
Notes	

Website	
Username	
Password	
Email	
Notes	

Website	
Username	
Password	
Email	
Notes	

Website	
Username	
Password	
Email	
Notes	

Website	
Username	
Password	
Email	
Notes	

STUFF I CAN'T REMEMBER

W

Website	
Username	
Password	
Email	
Notes	

Website	
Username	
Password	
Email	
Notes	

Website	
Username	
Password	
Email	
Notes	

Website	
Username	
Password	
Email	
Notes	

Website	
Username	
Password	
Email	
Notes	

Website	
Username	
Password	
Email	
Notes	

Website	
Username	
Password	
Email	
Notes	

Website	
Username	
Password	
Email	
Notes	

STUFF I CAN'T REMEMBER

Website	
Username	
Password	
Email	
Notes	

Website	
Username	
Password	
Email	
Notes	

Website	
Username	
Password	
Email	
Notes	

Website	
Username	
Password	
Email	
Notes	

Website	
Username	
Password	
Email	
Notes	

Website	
Username	
Password	
Email	
Notes	

Website	
Username	
Password	
Email	
Notes	

Website	
Username	
Password	
Email	
Notes	

STUFF I CAN'T REMEMBER

W

Website	
Username	
Password	
Email	
Notes	

Website	
Username	
Password	
Email	
Notes	

Website	
Username	
Password	
Email	
Notes	

Website	
Username	
Password	
Email	
Notes	

Website	
Username	
Password	
Email	
Notes	

Website	
Username	
Password	
Email	
Notes	

Website	
Username	
Password	
Email	
Notes	

Website	
Username	
Password	
Email	
Notes	

STUFF I CAN'T REMEMBER

Website	
Username	
Password	
Email	
Notes	

Website	
Username	
Password	
Email	
Notes	

Website	
Username	
Password	
Email	
Notes	

Website	
Username	
Password	
Email	
Notes	

Website	
Username	
Password	
Email	
Notes	

Website	
Username	
Password	
Email	
Notes	

Website	
Username	
Password	
Email	
Notes	

Website	
Username	
Password	
Email	
Notes	

STUFF I CAN'T REMEMBER

X

Website	
Username	
Password	
Email	
Notes	

Website	
Username	
Password	
Email	
Notes	

Website	
Username	
Password	
Email	
Notes	

Website	
Username	
Password	
Email	
Notes	

Website	
Username	
Password	
Email	
Notes	

Website	
Username	
Password	
Email	
Notes	

Website	
Username	
Password	
Email	
Notes	

Website	
Username	
Password	
Email	
Notes	

STUFF I CAN'T REMEMBER

Website	
Username	
Password	
Email	
Notes	

Website	
Username	
Password	
Email	
Notes	

Website	
Username	
Password	
Email	
Notes	

Website	
Username	
Password	
Email	
Notes	

Website	
Username	
Password	
Email	
Notes	

Website	
Username	
Password	
Email	
Notes	

Website	
Username	
Password	
Email	
Notes	

Website	
Username	
Password	
Email	
Notes	

STUFF I CAN'T REMEMBER

X

Website	
Username	
Password	
Email	
Notes	

Website	
Username	
Password	
Email	
Notes	

Website	
Username	
Password	
Email	
Notes	

Website	
Username	
Password	
Email	
Notes	

Website	
Username	
Password	
Email	
Notes	

Website	
Username	
Password	
Email	
Notes	

Website	
Username	
Password	
Email	
Notes	

Website	
Username	
Password	
Email	
Notes	

STUFF I CAN'T REMEMBER

Website	
Username	
Password	
Email	
Notes	

Website	
Username	
Password	
Email	
Notes	

Website	
Username	
Password	
Email	
Notes	

Website	
Username	
Password	
Email	
Notes	

Website	
Username	
Password	
Email	
Notes	

Website	
Username	
Password	
Email	
Notes	

Website	
Username	
Password	
Email	
Notes	

Website	
Username	
Password	
Email	
Notes	

STUFF I CAN'T REMEMBER

Website	
Username	
Password	
Email	
Notes	

Website	
Username	
Password	
Email	
Notes	

Website	
Username	
Password	
Email	
Notes	

Website	
Username	
Password	
Email	
Notes	

Website	
Username	
Password	
Email	
Notes	

Website	
Username	
Password	
Email	
Notes	

Website	
Username	
Password	
Email	
Notes	

Website	
Username	
Password	
Email	
Notes	

STUFF I CAN'T REMEMBER

Website	
Username	
Password	
Email	
Notes	

Website	
Username	
Password	
Email	
Notes	

Website	
Username	
Password	
Email	
Notes	

Website	
Username	
Password	
Email	
Notes	

Website	
Username	
Password	
Email	
Notes	

Website	
Username	
Password	
Email	
Notes	

Website	
Username	
Password	
Email	
Notes	

Website	
Username	
Password	
Email	
Notes	

STUFF I CAN'T REMEMBER

Y

Website	
Username	
Password	
Email	
Notes	

Website	
Username	
Password	
Email	
Notes	

Website	
Username	
Password	
Email	
Notes	

Website	
Username	
Password	
Email	
Notes	

Website	
Username	
Password	
Email	
Notes	

Website	
Username	
Password	
Email	
Notes	

Website	
Username	
Password	
Email	
Notes	

Website	
Username	
Password	
Email	
Notes	

STUFF I CAN'T REMEMBER

Website	
Username	
Password	
Email	
Notes	

Website	
Username	
Password	
Email	
Notes	

Website	
Username	
Password	
Email	
Notes	

Website	
Username	
Password	
Email	
Notes	

Website	
Username	
Password	
Email	
Notes	

Website	
Username	
Password	
Email	
Notes	

Website	
Username	
Password	
Email	
Notes	

Website	
Username	
Password	
Email	
Notes	

STUFF I CAN'T REMEMBER

Z

Website	
Username	
Password	
Email	
Notes	

Website	
Username	
Password	
Email	
Notes	

Website	
Username	
Password	
Email	
Notes	

Website	
Username	
Password	
Email	
Notes	

Website	
Username	
Password	
Email	
Notes	

Website	
Username	
Password	
Email	
Notes	

Website	
Username	
Password	
Email	
Notes	

Website	
Username	
Password	
Email	
Notes	

STUFF I CAN'T REMEMBER

Website	
Username	
Password	
Email	
Notes	

Website	
Username	
Password	
Email	
Notes	

Website	
Username	
Password	
Email	
Notes	

Website	
Username	
Password	
Email	
Notes	

Website	
Username	
Password	
Email	
Notes	

Website	
Username	
Password	
Email	
Notes	

Website	
Username	
Password	
Email	
Notes	

Website	
Username	
Password	
Email	
Notes	

STUFF I CAN'T REMEMBER

Website	
Username	
Password	
Email	
Notes	

Website	
Username	
Password	
Email	
Notes	

Website	
Username	
Password	
Email	
Notes	

Website	
Username	
Password	
Email	
Notes	

Website	
Username	
Password	
Email	
Notes	

Website	
Username	
Password	
Email	
Notes	

Website	
Username	
Password	
Email	
Notes	

Website	
Username	
Password	
Email	
Notes	

STUFF I CAN'T REMEMBER

Website	
Username	
Password	
Email	
Notes	

Website	
Username	
Password	
Email	
Notes	

Website	
Username	
Password	
Email	
Notes	

Website	
Username	
Password	
Email	
Notes	

Website	
Username	
Password	
Email	
Notes	

Website	
Username	
Password	
Email	
Notes	

Website	
Username	
Password	
Email	
Notes	

Website	
Username	
Password	
Email	
Notes	

STUFF I CAN'T REMEMBER

Website	
Username	
Password	
Email	
Notes	

Website	
Username	
Password	
Email	
Notes	

Website	
Username	
Password	
Email	
Notes	

Website	
Username	
Password	
Email	
Notes	

Website	
Username	
Password	
Email	
Notes	

Website	
Username	
Password	
Email	
Notes	

Website	
Username	
Password	
Email	
Notes	

Website	
Username	
Password	
Email	
Notes	

STUFF I CAN'T REMEMBER

Website	
Username	
Password	
Email	
Notes	

Website	
Username	
Password	
Email	
Notes	

Website	
Username	
Password	
Email	
Notes	

Website	
Username	
Password	
Email	
Notes	

Website	
Username	
Password	
Email	
Notes	

Website	
Username	
Password	
Email	
Notes	

Website	
Username	
Password	
Email	
Notes	

Website	
Username	
Password	
Email	
Notes	

STUFF I CAN'T REMEMBER

Website	
Username	
Password	
Email	
Notes	

Website	
Username	
Password	
Email	
Notes	

Website	
Username	
Password	
Email	
Notes	

Website	
Username	
Password	
Email	
Notes	

Website	
Username	
Password	
Email	
Notes	

Website	
Username	
Password	
Email	
Notes	

Website	
Username	
Password	
Email	
Notes	

Website	
Username	
Password	
Email	
Notes	

STUFF I CAN'T REMEMBER

Website	
Username	
Password	
Email	
Notes	

Website	
Username	
Password	
Email	
Notes	

Website	
Username	
Password	
Email	
Notes	

Website	
Username	
Password	
Email	
Notes	

Website	
Username	
Password	
Email	
Notes	

Website	
Username	
Password	
Email	
Notes	

Website	
Username	
Password	
Email	
Notes	

Website	
Username	
Password	
Email	
Notes	

STUFF I CAN'T REMEMBER

Website	
Username	
Password	
Email	
Notes	

Website	
Username	
Password	
Email	
Notes	

Website	
Username	
Password	
Email	
Notes	

Website	
Username	
Password	
Email	
Notes	

Website	
Username	
Password	
Email	
Notes	

Website	
Username	
Password	
Email	
Notes	

Website	
Username	
Password	
Email	
Notes	

Website	
Username	
Password	
Email	
Notes	

STUFF I CAN'T REMEMBER

Website	
Username	
Password	
Email	
Notes	

Website	
Username	
Password	
Email	
Notes	

Website	
Username	
Password	
Email	
Notes	

Website	
Username	
Password	
Email	
Notes	

Website	
Username	
Password	
Email	
Notes	

Website	
Username	
Password	
Email	
Notes	

Website	
Username	
Password	
Email	
Notes	

Website	
Username	
Password	
Email	
Notes	

STUFF I CAN'T REMEMBER

Website	
Username	
Password	
Email	
Notes	

Website	
Username	
Password	
Email	
Notes	

Website	
Username	
Password	
Email	
Notes	

Website	
Username	
Password	
Email	
Notes	

Website	
Username	
Password	
Email	
Notes	

Website	
Username	
Password	
Email	
Notes	

Website	
Username	
Password	
Email	
Notes	

Website	
Username	
Password	
Email	
Notes	

STUFF I CAN'T REMEMBER

Website	
Username	
Password	
Email	
Notes	

Website	
Username	
Password	
Email	
Notes	

Website	
Username	
Password	
Email	
Notes	

Website	
Username	
Password	
Email	
Notes	

Website	
Username	
Password	
Email	
Notes	

Website	
Username	
Password	
Email	
Notes	

Website	
Username	
Password	
Email	
Notes	

Website	
Username	
Password	
Email	
Notes	

STUFF I CAN'T REMEMBER

Website	
Username	
Password	
Email	
Notes	

Website	
Username	
Password	
Email	
Notes	

Website	
Username	
Password	
Email	
Notes	

Website	
Username	
Password	
Email	
Notes	

Website	
Username	
Password	
Email	
Notes	

Website	
Username	
Password	
Email	
Notes	

Website	
Username	
Password	
Email	
Notes	

Website	
Username	
Password	
Email	
Notes	

STUFF I CAN'T REMEMBER

Website	
Username	
Password	
Email	
Notes	

Website	
Username	
Password	
Email	
Notes	

Website	
Username	
Password	
Email	
Notes	

Website	
Username	
Password	
Email	
Notes	

Website	
Username	
Password	
Email	
Notes	

Website	
Username	
Password	
Email	
Notes	

Website	
Username	
Password	
Email	
Notes	

Website	
Username	
Password	
Email	
Notes	

STUFF I CAN'T REMEMBER

Website	
Username	
Password	
Email	
Notes	

Website	
Username	
Password	
Email	
Notes	

Website	
Username	
Password	
Email	
Notes	

Website	
Username	
Password	
Email	
Notes	

Website	
Username	
Password	
Email	
Notes	

Website	
Username	
Password	
Email	
Notes	

Website	
Username	
Password	
Email	
Notes	

Website	
Username	
Password	
Email	
Notes	

STUFF I CAN'T REMEMBER

Website	
Username	
Password	
Email	
Notes	

Website	
Username	
Password	
Email	
Notes	

Website	
Username	
Password	
Email	
Notes	

Website	
Username	
Password	
Email	
Notes	

Website	
Username	
Password	
Email	
Notes	

Website	
Username	
Password	
Email	
Notes	

Website	
Username	
Password	
Email	
Notes	

Website	
Username	
Password	
Email	
Notes	

STUFF I CAN'T REMEMBER

Website	
Username	
Password	
Email	
Notes	

Website	
Username	
Password	
Email	
Notes	

Website	
Username	
Password	
Email	
Notes	

Website	
Username	
Password	
Email	
Notes	

Website	
Username	
Password	
Email	
Notes	

Website	
Username	
Password	
Email	
Notes	

Website	
Username	
Password	
Email	
Notes	

Website	
Username	
Password	
Email	
Notes	

STUFF I CAN'T REMEMBER

Website	
Username	
Password	
Email	
Notes	

Website	
Username	
Password	
Email	
Notes	

Website	
Username	
Password	
Email	
Notes	

Website	
Username	
Password	
Email	
Notes	

Website	
Username	
Password	
Email	
Notes	

Website	
Username	
Password	
Email	
Notes	

Website	
Username	
Password	
Email	
Notes	

Website	
Username	
Password	
Email	
Notes	